ISBN 978-0-282-01474-2
PIBN 10840405

This book is a reproduction of an important historical work. Forgotten Books uses state-of-the-art technology to digitally reconstruct the work, preserving the original format whilst repairing imperfections present in the aged copy. In rare cases, an imperfection in the original, such as a blemish or missing page, may be replicated in our edition. We do, however, repair the vast majority of imperfections successfully; any imperfections that remain are intentionally left to preserve the state of such historical works.

English
Français
Deutsche
Italiano
Español
Português

www.forgottenbooks.com

Mythology Photography **Fiction**
Fishing Christianity **Art** Cooking
Essays Buddhism Freemasonry
Medicine **Biology** Music **Ancient
Egypt** Evolution Carpentry Physics
Dance Geology **Mathematics** Fitness
Shakespeare **Folklore** Yoga Marketing
Confidence Immortality Biographies
Poetry **Psychology** Witchcraft
Electronics Chemistry History **Law**
Accounting **Philosophy** Anthropology
Alchemy Drama Quantum Mechanics
Atheism Sexual Health **Ancient History**
Entrepreneurship Languages Sport
Paleontology Needlework Islam
Metaphysics Investment Archaeology
Parenting Statistics Criminology
Motivational

Stars of Destiny

The Ancient Science of Astrology

and How to Make Use of it Today

BY

TRIX DEVOS

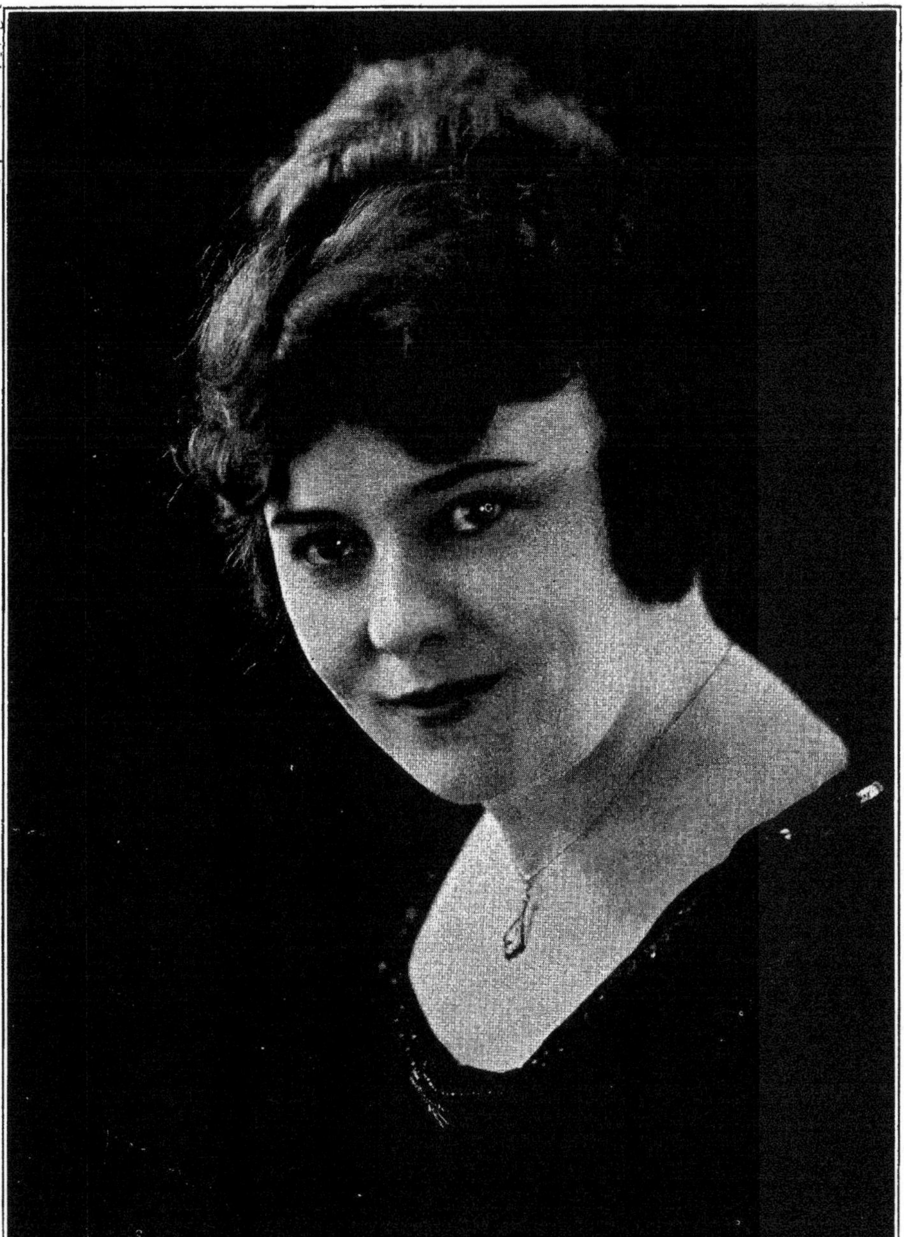

C. A. KIRCHHOFF

It is gratifying to know that Professor Chas. A Kirchhoff is one of the most intelligent Astrologers. He has a host of ardent and zealous friends who appreciate him for his integrity as well as for his ability, devotion and enthusiasm, which is not diminishing in the slightest degree.

ASTROLOGY

Astrology is the science of delineating character and judging past, present and future events from the positions of the planets and of the earth in the Zodiac at any given time. It is the key that opens to seekers after knowledge an explanation of the mysterious and unchanging laws that govern the universe and all living things. Astrology has interested the most advanced races of mankind ever since the reflective faculties of the mind were developed which is evidenced by recorded history and research into the manners and costumes of past ages. There is more in Astrology than the mere writing and reading of horoscopes and the delineating of character and vocations, which the casual reader does not comprehend. The study of Astrology will develop talents that are latent and of which persons are unconscious. It will intensify natural intuition and makes perceptible things which would otherwise have remained obscured. There are two motives in the student taking up the study of Astrology. The first is to thoroughly understand one's own nature. The second is to become of use to those who do not have the advantage and opportunity of obtaining this knowledge for themselves.

No one should hesitate to begin an investigation of this science for even a superficial examination will show that there is a way, in the apparent inequality of mankind. It will show why some persons succeed and others fail. Why some are weak, and others strong. Why some persons continually quarrel while with others there is peace, quiet and harmony. Sickly sentiment and distaste for improving the mind is inculcated by reading stupid books and vulgar novels so by the study of the science of Astrology is the mind expanded, new and ever rising ideas and thoughts are elevated and the pleasures of life realized.

If the science of Astrology was sufficiently known very many of the evils now afflicting mankind would not prevail and much pain, sorrow, trouble and consequent disappointment now abounding would not exist. Never before in the history of the world has the struggle for existence been so demoralized and unsettled. Therefore it behooves every sensible, thinking man and woman to grasp every means and opportunity to better their conditions by permanent efforts to rise to the higher places of thought and action.

Invisible things cannot be seen, yet invisible things such as gas, the producing power of the Sun, the vital power of plants, and animals, thought feeling, psychological influence, electricity and many other things too numerous to mention, are never the less facts and exist in spite of the incapacity of ordinary persons to explain them.* The person who denies the existence of anything beyond his comprehension is as credulous as one who believes everything without discrimination. Both of these persons are slaves to opinion or limited in their intercourse with the world. That a practical Astrologer can select these times with unerring accuracy has been proven by hundreds of years testimony in that direction. The man who dares not follow his own judgments, but constantly takes the advice of others, becomes at last a moral weakling and an intellectual dwarf. He is, in fact, a mere fragment of a human being, carried about the world, an insignificant cipher. A sober, industrious person with fair abilities may fail at times by following his judgment, but such a person must eventually succeed. Know your work, then do it.

Astrology is the science which teaches the effect of the planets on Human Life and the things of the Earth. By it we can foretell future events according to the position of the heavenly bodies at the time of birth.

That it is the oldest Science in existence is proved by the fact that the Astrological Signs have been found in ancient Temples, known to be more than ten thousand years old. I can not emphasize too strongly that Astrology is not Universal because the mentality of the people is not there to grasp the meaning of the science. Astrology today is based on sound mathematical calculations, the

2

The National Astrological Society

of the

United States ✠

[INCORPORATED]

This is to Certify that

Mrs. J. A. Davis

has been duly admitted as an Ordinary Member in the National Astrological Society of the United States, a Religious Society, incorporated under the Laws of the State of Minnesota, September 14, 1909, and by vote of the Annual Convention of January 6, 1915, removed to, and reincorporated under the Laws of the State of Massachusetts.

Signed:

Frank J. Seabright, D.A., President.

Walter W. Lewis, D.A., Secretary.

Dated *December 11* 1916.

INFLUENCE OF PLANETS IN THE MUNDANE HOUSES.

NOTE—Read carefully!

Before taking literally, word for word, the delineations follo..· ing, first see if the planet in question is in any dignity or debility, and in good or bad aspect, and to what natured planets, and from what Houses; then modify the reading accordingly.

These interpretations are for the planets unaspected and by their positions in the Houses alone, unless otherwise stated. If a planet is aspected by another, its delineation by House, as herein given, is subject to modification correspondingly.

For instance: "Saturn in the Fifth House."

"Delay, disappointment and sorrow through love affairs, affections and pleasures; incapacity for obtaining real enjoyment; loss through speculations, investments."

Now, if Saturn were in Capricorn, the Sign it rules, and well aspected or free from affliction, it would not be near so bad, giving an attraction for a serious, elderly person; quiet enjoyment; success in investment in lands, mines and property, lead, coal and such things as Saturn rules.

By taking this idea into consideration and giving your own modified interpretation, even if you only give ten words, using this as a guide, you bring into unfoldment the latent faculties of perception and expression, besides developing judgment and intuition. Notice the nature of the planet; note the nature of the Sign in which it is located; see if it is at home or at ease therein; then look up its aspects and you are ready to blend and modify according to the testimonies thus gathered.

Planets in House are indications only and do not give continued success or continued difficulty.

the body ruled by the Sign it is in. Bruises to the head. The nature is reserved, thoughtful, mistrustful, subtle, acquisitive and careful of personal affairs, secretive and given to periods of gloom and discontent.

Loss and misfortune through negligence, habits, lack of opportunity, or fateful events and delays.

It also indicates many sorrows and disappointments, sometimes poverty, and an uphill time generally.

Saturn rules the bones, teeth, right ear, knees and spleen; gives a liability to suffer from colds, chills and poor circulation, also through constipation, rheumatism, stone, gravel, obstructed growth and deficient action.

Uranus in First House.

Uranus signifies originality of thought, independence of mind, inventive genius, intuition, intellectual and metaphysical ability. It predisposes one to the occult, the antiquated, old, curious new and the odd, in fact to everything out of the ordinary.

It attracts towards such subject as Astrology, phrenology, occultism, mesmerism, hypnotism, spiritualism, psychic research, magnetic healing, telepathy, psychism, Free Masonry, inventions, electricity, etc.

It makes one appear odd, peculiar, eccentric, progressive and about one hundred years ahead of their time.

It is significant of many changes in residence and occupation and is usually not good here for marriage, bringing about peculiar, unfortunate conditions, difficulties and separations.

It is Uranus manifesting which makes one independent and revolutionary, apt to change thoughts and position radically and suddenly, forming his own opinions regardless of what others may think of them. Estrangements from parents and kindred.

Uranus stands for freedom, equality, and its natives can always see how conditions may be better, even when they are almost well enough in the opinion of many. They are nearly always on the opposite to the things that are popular, formal or limited, preferring expansion and upheaval, and therefore takes the side of the unpopular in movements, studies, sciences, religion, etc. He is often called a crank, but invariably his cranky notions become accepted facts after a time. They are usually forceful, but not particularly quarrelsome or antagonistic, but are vigorous in the cause of the oppressed. They are not at all opposed to discussion or debate and seldom become angry in it; detest limitations and cannot stand control or dictation.

Uranus rules the originating or creating faculties, phrenologically expressed, the faculties of comparison and casualty, without which there can be no invention or science.

While Uranus gives originality and individuality of thought, yet one may be running over with good ideas, but unless Mercury assists he will never get them uttered satisfactorily.

Mercury gives the ability to reason, understand, interpret, expound and express. "And I will send Aaron (Mercury) thy brother, for I know he can speak well, but thou Moses (Uranus) shall teach him what to say."

The enlightened Uranian gives all the freedom possible to those around him, knowing that his liberty is increased correspondingly. However, just how fine the native will manifest or interpret the rays from Uranus depends upon the quality of the ASPECTS to it in the chart.

Uranus afflicted shows quickness of mind, mental impulsiveness, originality, independence and self-will, changeful, impulsive, abrupt, erratic, eccentric, wilful, brusque, sarcastic, critical and easily offended; inventive genius.

It gives unconventionality, irregularity, strange ideas, separations, estrangements, journeys, sudden changes and losses in unexpected ways.

. ‾ Danger through lightning, electricity and hurts by machinery, inventions, engines, explosions and vehicles of travel. Mysterious happenings. Gives an interest in all occult affairs and rules the psychic aura and the personal magnetism.

Neptune in First House.

The influence of this planet is always more or less mediumistic and the native will either consciously or unconsciously take on the conditions of the surroundings and of those with whom they come in contact. It being a neutral planet, it depends upon ASPECTS for the manner in which it will manifest.

It represents inspiration, trance, dreams, weird feelings, thoughts and experiences. Romance and emotion. Visionary mind.

When well aspected it gives good intuition and spirit perceptions; ruling the organ of calculation it denotes far-seeing, able to estimate quickly and accurately. It attracts one to peculiar people, psychic centers and mysterious, strange places.

It gives ability to cultivate thought reading and transference, clairvoyance, crystal gazing, psychometry, etc.

It exalts the artistic tastes, giving a love for beauty in form, color and sound. It bears relation to matters connected with the sea, water and liquids in general, also mediumship and Spiritualism. When it is weak or afflicted it seems to open an avenue of temptation that appeals to the passional, sense-loving and emotional side of the nature, bringing uncertainty and confusion through instability, indolence or lack of energy. Danger through plots, schemes, enmities and deceptions.

While it indicates intuition, enthusiasm and perception, yet it denotes a receptivity to the psychic conditions that might run into extremes, allowing the feelings to get the upper hand of the judgment; excitability, changefulness, imagination, strange or unnatural appetites, intrigues, acts of indiscretion, deceptions, assumings, love of luxury and taste; wandering disposition, many jour-

23

neys, changes, up and downs. Being rapidly affected by the environments or surrounding conditions psychically, mentally and physically; they should investigate the philosophy of all things mysterious rather than the phenomena.

There are days when Neptune people should have nothing to do whatever with any occult phenomena, seances or drugs, medicines, gases, etc., and, again, there are days when they should strive to develop their occult faculties. These times are when other planets come into aspect with Neptune, particularly the Moon.

SECOND HOUSE.

Moon in Second House.

Gain by employment, through public affairs and occupations, by dealing with liquids and commodities, and the wants of the common people generally. Money obtained through females or the mother. Good for things ruled by the Moon and the Sign it is in.

If well aspected it is favorable for financial success, although somewhat variable.

Mercury in Second House.

Denotes gain by letters, writings, speaking, traveling, teaching, clerking, commissions and ordinary business and commercial affairs generally, also through study, advertising, distributing, stationery, books, etc. Gain through any occupation according to the nature of the planet in closest good aspect.

Venus in Second House.

By luck and good will and favors from others money comes readily, it is often gained through artistic pursuits, music, pleasure, social affairs, friendships, societies, marriage, jewelry, millinery, hotels, confectionery and wearing apparel.

A good deal of money is spent on adornment, luxuries, pleasure, friends, etc., but nevertheless they get it to spend.

Sun in Second House.

Money obtained by industrious effort and through the father and superiors; gain by affairs of government or through holding official appointments or other responsible positions. Benefit

24

tion to mesmeric or magnetic healing. The mind is curious, inventive, ingenious, unconventional and fond of the occult, mystical, new, extraordinary, profound, ancient or unpopular studies and social or mental reforms. Intuitive perception and understanding with regard to things occult. If Uranus is afflicted by Saturn, or Mars, it shows danger of accidents, wrecks or explosions on journeys, through vehicles of travel or treachery on the part of relatives.

If afflicted by Moon or Mercury, the native incurs severe criticism on account of his ideas, projects and mental attitude.

Neptune in Third House.

Denotes psychological faculties; spiritual perception; fruitful, inventive mind, given to the investigation of spirit phenomena and matters pertaining to the occult or mysterious.

It gives inspirational ideas and weird feelings or experiences. Signifies journeys, peculiar difficulties with relatives, schemes, plots, deceits, etc. Changes in name—nick-name, nom de plume or alias.

If Neptune is weak or badly aspected it is not good for the mind, showing hallucinations, morbid fancies, imbecility, weak intellect or depraved tastes.

When well aspected it gives artistic taste or appreciation of an exalted order through a peculiar blending of the feelings and intuitions, and ability to get beautiful things inspirationally; possibility of independent or automatic writings, etc.

FOURTH HOUSE.

Moon in Fourth House.

Well placed or aspected, it shows gain and benefit through the parents, home and domestic life; favors from the opposite sex, some chance of inheritance. Publicity or popularity through the parents; many changes in residence and fluctuation in affairs towards the close of life. If well dignified here it shows ultimate rise to success and independence. Possessions and prosperity.

But if Saturn afflicts the Moon great difficulty will be encountered in attaining success, or, in fact, keeping from poverty and sorrow through family affairs. Afflictions by Mars, Sun or Mercury denotes loss by theft, fraud or deception. Jupiter adverse denotes lack of opportunities and limitations through environments. Uranus adverse: sudden changes; difficulties with home affairs; estrangements from or loss of parents, probably the mother; loss through unexpected reversals and changes. Neptune adverse: mystery or complications concerning home affairs.

Mercury in Fourth House.

Inconstancy in affairs generally; change of residence through matters connected with business; often the subject has no fixed abode; many traveling men have this position.

Worry and anxiety regarding disturbance in home affairs.

Good position for proprietors of private schools or other stationary places where literary or clerical work is carried on, such as land, mine and real estate agencies, registry offices, newspaper offices, libraries, publishers, etc.

In bad aspect to Uranus, difficulty through the mind at the close of life or sudden end.

Saturn adverse: denotes deception, fraud and theft.

Mars adverse: loss through imposition and controversy.

Sun, Moon or Jupiter adverse: lack of opportunity or limitations.

Uranus in good aspect: occult investigations and enlightenment before the close of life.

Saturn or Jupiter in good aspect: steadier, more satisfied and studious; inclines to success, opportunities and inheritance.

Sun, Moon or Venus in good aspect: activity, popularity and success before the close of life.

Venus in Fourth House.

Indicative of favorable domestic affairs and happiness through the parents; love of home and country. Chance of gain by inheritance, parents, houses or property and investment; peaceful, com-

30

fortable conditions at the close of life. Successful termination to hopes and wishes. Sun, Moon or Jupiter in good aspect is exceedingly fortunate, bringing general affairs to a successful issue.

In good aspect to Uranus or Saturn : success in old age.

The adverse aspects of Sun, Moon, Mercury or Jupiter are not particularly evil, but affect the finances.

Mars adverse: difficulty through generosity, carelessness or extravagance toward the close of life.

Saturn, Uranus or Neptune adverse: sudden, peculiar losses, disappointments and sorrows toward the end of life.

Sun in Fourth House.

A chance of honor in declining years, successful ambitions; hopes and wishes realized. Good for house, land, property and occupations connected with them. Gain or chance of inheritance by or through the parents; fortunate heredity.

Inclines to secrecy or investigation of occult or spiritual affairs; some psychic experiences.

In good aspect to Moon, Venus, Jupiter, Saturn or Uranus: gain; property; inheritance; financial success.

If afflicted: obstacles, limitations, troubles and sorrows through the parents and home life; liability to loss and difficulty by living beyond the means or through heavy obligations. Weakens the constitution at close of life.

Mars in Fourth House.

Domestic unpleasantness and many misunderstandings, inharmonies or quarrels in the home life, especially if Mercury afflicts. Losses by thefts, fire and accidents in the dwelling place; early death of a parent. Many difficulties, disappointments and obstacles. Worry in old age. Physical unpleasantness caused by bad digestion. Liability to loss through speculations in property, lands and mines. If Uranus or Saturn afflicts: danger of mental trouble, suicide or sudden end by accident, distress and poverty; unfortunate in the place of birth. The good aspects give much energy, force, activity and enterprise in the acquisition of possessions.

31

Jupiter in Fourth House.

Tends to satisfactory, comfortable and peaceful domestic affairs; successful home life and family surroundings; gain and favor through the parents, benefit through land and possessions; good position, property and success toward the close of life.

If unafflicted: A fortunate, easy life; success at the place of birth, successful termination to business enterprise and affairs generally.

Jupiter afflicted gives trouble through the parents or their affairs, and extravagance; heredity limitations.

Sun or Moon adverse: liability to sudden heart trouble or apoplexy.

Mercury adverse: danger of lawsuits over property or inheritance, and if both afflict, the ruler of the fourth: law with or through the parents. Mars or Saturn in good aspect: a religious or satisfactory end. Uranus favorable: occult tendencies; long life. The luminaries favorable: overcomes many adverse testimonies in the chart and shows a rise in life to opulence and popularity.

Saturn in Fourth House.

Difficulties and troubles through property, inheritance or mines. Sorrow through parents, probably the father. Acquisitiveness. Unsatisfactory domestic or home life. Much work, heavy responsibilities and great difficulty to success. Unfortunate in the place of birth. Seclusiveness at close of life.

If afflicted: denotes limitations, inability to bring affairs to satisfactory conclusions; poverty, privations. Parents or domestic affairs serve as a brake or "hold-back."

Good aspects, however, show a chance of inheritance and success by judicious investment in property, lands and mines; religious studies; serious nature; occult development; retiring disposition at the close of life.

Uranus in Fourth House.

Unsettled residence; many changes; a checkered career. Unfortunate in the place of birth. Estrangements from parents; domestic troubles and family affairs. Exceptional experiences. A sudden or peculiar end to life. Much work and strange or unexpected results. Worry through occupation; difficulty with employers or superiors. Loss of inheritance, if one is expected. Many ups and downs and tastes' of poverty through peculiar circumstances. Strong attraction to things occult.

Afflicted by the luminaries: liability to heart trouble and paralysis. Mercury adverse: mental derangements. Mars adverse: danger of violence. Saturn adverse: liability to accident. Neptune adverse: threatens loss through theft, fraud and deception, and accident by flood or action of the elements. Jupiter adverse: loss through Government matters, law or by lightning.

Neptune in Fourth House.

Changes of residence. Voyages. Peculiar domestic and family affairs, some secrets of mystery regarding the home life'; schemes, frauds and misunderstandings afflict the parents in some way. Unfavorable close of life in exile or seclusion; probability of being restraint or in a hospital or public institution. Psychic experiences. Much depends on the aspects. The luminaries in affliction: denotes weakened vitality and poor health. Mercury adverse: mental troubles and peculiar nervous disorders. Neptune is neutral, consequently good aspects would show benefits through property and houses, according to the nature of the aspects.

FIFTH HOUSE.

Moon in Fifth House.

Public success in connection with places of amusement or with women, children and young people; happy disposition; fondness for pleasure and the society of children and the opposite sex. Strong tendencies toward speculation. Much activity and change in all enterprise; changeable affections (except in Fixed Signs), yet the heart may be given to one who least deserves it and thus the affection change to aversion, coldness or indifference.

Several offspring (if in a Fruitful Sign).

It is indicative of a child who achieves fame and popularity, if well aspected, also that the native will in some manner be closely connected or drawn to a child or young person.

If the Moon is afflicted it brings loss through speculations, and danger or sorrow and trouble through love, children and morals.

Mercury in Fifth. House.

Refines the pleasures and makes them more mental than muscular, i. e., more of the mind than of the senses, and is good for occupations connected with entertainment, schools or travel.

This position denotes worry, anxiety and sorrow through objects of affection, and children and their affairs.

A good aspect of Saturn or Jupiter much improves the position and brings success and gain through these things and also through speculation, investment, etc. Luminaries favorable: indicates success in connection with traveling for public amusement and with children. Mars or Uranus adverse: Denotes troublesome love affairs, scandal, separations, divorce, lawsuits, etc.

Venus in Fifth House.

A fruitful union and handsome children who will be endowed with artistic or musical ability; happiness, comfort and gain through offspring, which are usually or mostly girls.

This position denotes gain and success through love affairs, friendships, etc., ability to entertain others and enjoy success through all manner of social intercourse, pleasure and amusement.

It indicates gain through speculation, investment and general enterprise, also through theatres, concerts, singing, music, painting, children, schools, etc.

If Venus is much afflicted it gives liability of injury to the health through over-indulgence in pleasurable gratifications. Saturn adverse: sorrow and disappointment through love, speculation, children, etc. Mars or Uranus adverse: trouble and danger through the opposite sex, and careless, rash, indiscriminative or unconventional bestowal of affection.

Sun in Fifth House.

Honorable and successful attachments. Gain through speculations, investments, enterprise, children, pleasure and places of amusement. Small family. This position often denies children

34

and produces difficult or dangerous child-birth; this, however, depends upon the nature of the Sign on the Cusp, whether barren or not, etc. If the Sun is afflicted here it causes loss through speculations, troubles and jealousy in courtship, and sorrow through love, pleasure and pride.

Mars in Fifth House.

Pleasure through the strenuous sports, athletics, muscular exercise. Impulsive, rash and unfortunate attractions towards the opposite sex. Sensual emotions or over-ardent affections and too much indulgence in pleasure, amusement and tastes results in physical, financial and social loss; danger of accident to first child. In a woman's horoscope this position shows difficult and dangerous child-birth. Loss by speculation, gaming, extravagance, pleasure and excess of feeling. Trouble with or through children.

Uranus, Saturn, Jupiter, Sun, Moon or Venus adverse: threatens danger of ruin or disgrace through the opposite sex.

Well aspected: gain through occupations and enterprise connected with pleasure and investment corresponding to the nature of Mars.

Jupiter in Fifth House.

Good and dutiful children, who will be a help and comfort to to the native. Success, happiness and gain through love affairs, and the opposite sex. Pleasure, success and gain in connection with places of amusement, theaters, socials, schools, etc. A good position for gain through speculation, investment and financial enterprise, more especially if Mars or Sun is in good aspect. For a female it denotes an attachment with an older gentleman or widower or to one of religious nature or social standing. Increases the number of children and is fortunate for them. If Jupiter is afflicted it modifies its good influence, giving the same desires but troubles, losses and obstacles, according to the nature of the afflicting planet and from which House.

Saturn in Fifth House.

Denotes disappointments, delays, hindrance and sorrow in connection with love affairs; attraction to those who are older or more serious in disposition.

Loss of child and troubles and unhappiness through children.

Loss by speculation, investment and games of chance.

Danger from hurts by animals while on pleasure.

Danger of drowning if Saturn is in Scorpio, and of heart trouble if in Leo. If Saturn is well aspected by either Sun or Moon and not otherwise afflicted, it is a good position for investment in lands, mines and property and such things which Saturn governs. If afflicted by Sun, Moon or Jupiter, take no chances of any kind.

Uranus in Fifth House.

Unconventional ideas with regard to sex union; strange, romantic, inconstant, secret or impulsive love affairs. Social vexations, scandal, etc.

Loss of first child through some sudden or extraordinary manner or separation, anxiety and trouble through children; difficulty through child-birth. Difficulties in domestic life and love attachments. Loss through speculation, risks, chances, etc. Liking for all odd, new, daring pleasures or places of amusement.

Neptune in Fifth House.

Strange and peculiar experiences in connection with the feelings, emotions and affections; abnormal conditions relating to sex matters. Sensuous pleasures. Seduction. If afflicted it denotes trouble. faithlessness or confusion and sorrow in love affairs and loss through lax control of the desires and appetites; losses in speculation through deceit or treachery. If well aspected the native will be benefited in his development through a fortunate union with one of the opposite sex; gain by investment in oil, shipping and such things as Neptune rules.

SIXTH HOUSE.

Moon in Sixth House.

Uncertain health, especially in a woman's horoscope; much sickness and danger in infancy. Desire to serve the public in some professional capacity. The subject has better knack and ability of getting good results from serving others than from others serving him. Many changes among servants or employes. Success in domestic service or in catering to the public's want for necessities, food stuffs, drinks, etc.

Good aspects to the Moon helps the health and gives success with small animals, servants and through some subordinate position connected with the occupations ruled by the Sign the Moon occupies. Moon afflicted gives poor success with employes and treachery and dishonesty among them; bad for small animals, poultry, etc.; weakness in the part of the body ruled by the Sign Moon is in.

Afflicted in Common Signs: danger from lung trouble and chronic diseases. Fixed Signs: bronchitis, gravel or stone. Cardinal Signs: nervous derangements and stomach trouble.

Moon afflicted by Mercury: indigestion, aches in head and teeth; bowel troubles.

Moon afflicted by Venus: functional or skin trouble.

Moon afflicted by Mars: inflammatory complaints.

Moon afflicted by Jupiter: liver and blood trouble.

Moon afflicted by Saturn: chronic diseases; poor circulation.

Moon afflicted by Sun, Uranus or Neptune: weak vitality; indigestion; indisposition through psychic conditions.

Mercury in Sixth House.

Many small vexations through servants; journeys on account of health. Good position for the study of hygiene, medicine or chemistry. Gain in subordinate positions through writings, clerical work and Mercurial affairs generally.

Active mentality, but liable to become overstrung or impaired through anxiety, worry or overwork, causing dyspepsia or a tendency to become easily affected by the surrounding conditions.

37

Any afflictions to Mercury here are dangerous to the health through the mentality and nervous organization.

Afflicted by Uranus: liable to become unbalanced or commit suicide.

Afflicted by Saturn: danger through despondency or worry.

Afflicted by Mars: mental derangement or excitement.

Afflicted by Sun, Moon, or Neptune: fevers, stomach trouble; indisposition through psychic conditions.

Venus in Sixth House.

Is favorable to good health, but care and discretion should be exercised to keep from excesses of all kinds, especially with regard to eating and drinking. Gain in the employ of others. It is favorable for success and benefits through servants, hygiene, medicine, nursing, and by clothing, small animals, poultry, etc. People with Venus here often take up work for the pleasure it gives them and the interest it creates. Love for pets, fine clothes and adornments. If afflicted it shows trouble to the health through indulgences, and to that part of the body ruled by the Sign Venus is in or by the planet afflicting. Health improves after marriage.

Sun in Sixth House.

This is a cadent House, therefore the Sun, ruler of vitality, placed here is not in a very good position for health, as it may slightly weaken the constitution. If afflicted by Neptune, Uranus or Saturn, the recuperative power is not good, and a great deal of indisposition will be encountered; liability to contagious diseases and danger from epidemics.

When the Sun is well aspected the native seems to intuitively understand how to safeguard the health and in that way escapes ills.

Any aspect of Mars strengthens the constitution.

A good aspect of Mars, Jupiter or Venus would show success and gain through servants and service rendered; success, promotion and fortunate conditions in employments that benefit others, such as healing, doctoring, chemistry, hospital work, etc., in fact, the Sun well dignified or aspected here indicates that the native can do a great work in assisting to relieve the sufferings of humanity.

38

Sun afflicted in Fixed Signs: quinsy, bronchitis, asthma, diphtheria, gravel, heart trouble, weak back, sides and loins. Afflicted in Common Signs: chronic diseases, troubles with breathing organs. Afflicted in Cardinal Signs: liver trouble, nervousness, weak chest and stomach, rheumatism; also liable to some permanent injury.

Mars in Sixth House.

Disputes, quarrels, losses and thefts through servants or employes and much difficulty and annoyance by their taking liberties, advantages, etc. The native is usually an active, energetic and enthusiastic worker and liable to overdo himself, especially in the employ of others.

Mars rules the tastes and the subject is liable to impair, injure, or suffer in health through excesses, acts of indiscretion, carelessness, extravagance and through accident.

Its position here is usually significant of incision with steel to that part of the body ruled by the Sign it is in.

Mars afflicted: inflammation or accidents to that part of the body ruled by the Sign occupied; difficulty in employ; danger, loss and trouble through employes, animals, poultry, pets, etc.

Mars gives a tendency to inflammatory complaints in the bowels and troubles that part of the body represented by the·Sign occupied in about the same manner as does the Sun when in Sixth House and in a like Sign. (See Sun in Sixth House.)

Saturn adverse: danger of death through operations and animals.

Uranus adverse: danger of fatal accident or suicide.

Neptune adverse: danger of foul play, accidental poisoning, etc.

Jupiter in Sixth House.

Gives good health, and, if indisposed, the subject receives kind treatment, good attention and many comforts, in fact, is likely to gain through sickness. The native's care and presence would be beneficial and healing to others in distress.

If the person should become a physician, would be successful financially, and with the patients.

39

Gain and profit through employment, especially in high circles; also through servants and inferiors, and through religious, philanthropical and social tendencies. Success with small animals, poultry, etc. If afflicted the health will suffer from over-indulgence or intemperance in diet, and with the che t, bowels, liver, blood and digestive organs.

Saturn in Sixth House.

Denotes much sickness, through exposure and circumstances over which the subject has little control, neglect, privation, sorrow, disappointment, etc. Many lost opportunities through the state of health. Troubles according to the nature of the Sign Saturn occupies, something the same as Sun in Sixth House.

Not a good position for employment or success with servants or inferiors, denoting loss and trouble through them.

Ill success and loss with small animals, etc.

Afflicted by Uranus: incurable diseases.

Afflicted by Mars: dangerous illness through accident.

Afflicted by Sun, Moon or Neptune: chronic ill health, poor circulation and recuperation, colds, rheumatism, psychic and heavy ills. Notice the part of the body represented by the Sign occupied.

Saturn denotes poor digestion, constipation, obstruction, poor circulation, debility, etc., physics should not be administered, but instead, warm water enemas; physics rack and deplete the system in the performance of their work, while water benefits and is productive of better results.

Uranus in Sixth House.

Troubles through peculiar nervous disorders. Sickness which is puzzling or not well understood. If much afflicted the sicknesses are incurable; danger of mental derangements; danger of illness through the employment and through sudden changes. Not a good position for occupation, service, servants, employes, poultry, etc.

Treatment by electricity, mesmerism, hypnotism, etc., are apt to prove detrimental (if Uranus is afflicted, but beneficial if well aspected), and a careful study of the diet and environments should be made.

Uranus rules the aura and sometimes the subjects take on or sense the conditions of the person who prepares or handles the food and the influence might be adverse to them, or it might be good; investigate if you are having stomach trouble.

Never eat when tired, nervous, excited or angry. Uranus people especially should put on clothing for the first time only in the new of the Moon, and never wear any but their own.

If Uranus is well aspected here it may bring some unexpected or unique opportunity to perform exceptional service and obtain great results. Uranus well placed would give success as a metaphysician, and through occult and electric treatments.

Neptune in Sixth House.

Threatens some chronic, incurable disease, atrophy, inertia, wasting sickness, or some inherited tendencies. Danger of some deformity through illness. If much afflicted it shows severe sickness and danger from gratifying the tastes or desires, especially if afflicted by Mars. The subject should carefully avoid narcotics and opiates and if any medicine is taken use only the simplest kind, they will prove most efficacious. Neptune rules the mediumistic faculty, this house rules clothing, food, etc., consequently, the native should never take food into the stomach received from a sick person or one of undesirable habits, nor should any apparel be worn once used by another. Use only the most fresh and pure food obtainable and no animal matter. No success with poultry, etc. Thefts, schemes, plots, deceit, or loss and difficulty through servants.

This position may keep the native in seclusion, retirement or servitude. If well aspected the native can develop fine psychometrising powers, especially for sensing surrounding conditions. They should always pay attention to their own intuition in regard to food, clothing, environment, etc. Neptune people need to exercise great care regarding the physical condition and habits of their associates or of those whom they engage to treat them. Being genuinely receptive they absorb what others are throwing off and often this proves detrimental rather than beneficial, although the intentions may be good.

41

People who indulge in tobacco, liquors, or who countenance or encourage cruelty in any form, should never be allowed to touch the body of an indisposed Neptune person. Kindly suggestion, both verbal and mental, are best.

SEVENTH HOUSE.

Moon in Seventh House.

In a female chart it indicates a union with one whose affections are variable, fond of change and travel and of unsettled nature. If well aspected it favors an early marriage; partnership; public favor, popularity and social success, also money or property by marriage. Unless the Moon is well aspected and located this is not a favorable position; death of partner; public opposition and unpopularity; female enmity; trouble and loss through litigation; changeful relations with the opposite sex and with partner and associates. •

If the Moon is well aspected and to the ruler of the First House it helps to offset the adverse testimonies and magnify the good ones. In bad aspect to Mars: discord, discontent, hasty speech and action.

Saturn adverse: disappointment, loss and sorrows through unions.

Uranus adverse: separation, estrangement, peculiar experience* in connection with the unions; unexpected enmities.

Mercury adverse: matrimonial and business worries.

If the Moon is applying to any aspect of Uranus the native is likely to marry suddenly and meet one to whom affection is given afterwards. Taken alone: inclines to journeys and removals, especially when in a movable sign.

Mercury in Seventh House.

The native usually carries on Mercurial pursuits in partnership or association with others and is fortunate or otherwise thereby, according to aspects.

Unsettled married life; many inharmonies; the partner is quick in thought and action, and if afflicted, sarcastic, untruthful and hasty tempered; if well aspected, shrewd, active, clever and progressive. The partner is usually younger and oftentimes is an employe or is related in some way. Marriage is generally the result of writings or traveling and is more of the mind than of the senses or emotions. If Mercury is much afflicted: many small strifes, worries, vexations, through writings, speech, contracts, traveling, legal affairs, and business dealings with others.

Venus in Seventh House.

With marriage comes social and financial pleasures. The native usually marries early and enjoys much happiness; love for offspring; successful partnerships; peaceful termination to strifes and success in public relations.

If badly aspected it gives delay and sorrow in marriage; probably a dissipated partner; loss through litigation and partnerships.

Sun in Seventh House.

If well aspected success and rise in life after or through marriage; a proud but magnanimous, warm-hearted partner; firm and lasting attachment; happiness. Good for partnership and general popularity, especially with business people and superiors.

Difficulties averted by arbitration or mutual consent; gain through business, contracts and associations.

If afflicted: delays, opposition, disappointment, loss, etc., according to the nature of the planet aspecting.

Mars in Seventh House.

If afflicted: impetuous in love; an early or rash love affair or union; possible separation through excessive demonstration of affections and combative or forceful nature of partner. Death of partner.

In a female chart: danger of sudden death of husband or sudden accident to him. If Mars be in Cancer or Pisces he is apt to be worthless through dissipating habits.

In a male chart: the partner is industrious but assertive, posi-' tive or masculine.

Loss through litigation or partnership; business enemies; much strife, sometimes resulting in violence; criticism and opposition is frequently met. When Mars is well aspected if located by Sign much of the above is modified, the native may marry a Mars person and benefit thereby.

Jupiter in Seventh House.

If well aspected: success, gain and happiness through marriage, the partner being faithful and good.

The partner is usually of good social and financial standing; usually older, more patient, profound or religious than the native. Success in partnership and in dealing co-operatively with others; friends and popularity with and through business people; gain through litigation or legal affairs. Jupiter is weak in Virgo and Capricorn.

If afflicted by Uranus or Mars: loss by litigation is threatened.

Saturn or luminaries adverse: marriage is delayed or denied.

Saturn in Seventh House.

Well aspected or in Libra: gives a sincere, prudent, faithful and well-disposed partner, or union with one older and more serious than the native, not demonstrative or emotional, but stable in the affections, and possessing property.

If afflicted: grief, sorrow, death or enduring coldness on the part of the partner, who will be of Saturnine disposition and habit, according to the Sign and Aspects.

· Ruin by contracts and partnerships; persistent opponents; litigation; business enmities and treachery. Marriage about the age of 28 or after; incompatibility with the marriage partner.

Uranus in Seventh House.

Well aspected: union with one of genius, intuition, ability or original character.

A romantic, sudden, impulsive, secret or irregular union with likelihood of inharmonious results.

Taken alone: signifies voyages; life in foreign lands; legal or clerical persuasions. Keen, romantic, fanciful and idealistic mind. Some remarkable dream or psychic experiences. Fond of change, diversity and novelty. Publicity of some sort regarding science, religion, philosophy, traveling or mysticism.

Sun adverse: over-enthusiastic in religion, or unorthodox, probably both, at some time. Saturn adverse: sorrow and difficulty through religion, travel, publications, and partner's relatives. Uranus adverse: romantic, eccentric, fond of adventure; liberal religion.

Mercury in Ninth House.

Well aspected: literary ability, sharp, clever mentality; taste for art, science and all higher educational or enlightening subjects, love of knowledge, an ingenious, studious mind.

Success in journeys, clerical or legal affairs and publishing. Taken alone: a busy, active mind; danger of legal worries; taste for readings, science, literary pursuits and every form of knowledge. Desire for life in foreign countries, or travels to, and knowledge of, distant places.

Afflicted: tendency to worry and scatter forces by engaging in numerous things instead of concentrating on one until achieved; too much doubt; not enough decision; difficulties with clerical or legal affairs, fruitless and troublesome journeys.

Mercury in a Movable Sign is a sure indication of travels.

Venus in Ninth House.

Kind, sympathetic, helpful, gentle disposition and a cultured intellect; philosophical spirit; optimistic; appreciation for every form of mental improvement.

Fondness for fine arts, music, operas, high-class literature and lectures, social intercourse, and literary persons.

Benefits from relatives by marriage; pleasant journeys; success abroad. Venus here will modify many adverse testimonies regarding mental qualities and helps to keep the subject from harm.

The native may marry abroad or marry a foreigner or become united to one of a spiritual, scientific or artistic disposition.

49

If Venus is the highest planet in the map it is a splendid position, denoting honors, success, good marriage and good fortune generally. If Venus is afflicted it gives longings, high ideals and desires hard to materialize, and disappointments through their unattainment.

Sun in Ninth House.

Success or honors in connection with church, universities or law, also through travel and social intercourse; desire to investigate science and philosophy to find truths worthy of giving out to benefit others. Dignity or success abroad, or residence in foreign countries; faithful, earnest, sincere, consistent, and constant in religious beliefs whether orthodox or unconventional.

Ambitious spirit: firm, self-reliant and confident. Taste for fine arts, music, science and intellectual development.

Mars or Uranus afflicting: extreme, enthusiastic or peculiar in religious beliefs; troubles in foreign countries, also with legal affairs and partner's relations.

Jupiter adverse: unsuccessful in legal or clerical affairs.

Saturn adverse: hindrance through perversity, pride, etc., unsuccessful in clerical or legal affairs.

Jupiter favorable: success and honors through popular reasoning in science, religion or philosophy; a good counselor; favor of wife's relatives.

Saturn favorable: love for justice, ability for profound or responsible undertakings; philosophical.

Mars favorable: courageous and vigorous in defense of justice and right; patriotic.

Mars in Ninth House.

Many strifes, generally through legal or religious matters; danger of violence in foreign places; troubles through journeys and wife's relative. Distressful dreams or fancies.

Enthusiasm or impulse in religion or philosophy; liberality and freedom of thought. Forceful in beliefs.

If afflicted: forceful, fanatical, irregular or skeptical ideas regarding religious matters; preconceived or early religious teach-

50

ings are overthrown; many troubles; litigation; disputes; danger while traveling; disagreement with some of the relatives; changes of religion or indifference.

Well aspected: active in defense of rights; successful in law; enterprising in development.

Jupiter in Ninth House.

Well aspected: good intuition; clear foresight; success and honors in religious, collegiate, legal, philosophic or philanthropic affairs; favorable for travel and success abroad; prophetic faculty and prophetic dreams; peaceful, logical and optimistic disposition.

Mars adverse: danger of shipwreck, fire or accident through journeys, liability to extremes in religious matters, or trouble through them.

Uranus adverse: unexpected loss, difficulties and experiences through journeys, religion, law, philosophy, relatives, etc.

Mars or Uranus favorable: impulse towards occult philosophy, higher science, and originality of thought.

Saturn in Ninth House.

Well aspected: the mental attitude is scientific and philosophical, the nature is studious and meditative, given to the investigation of law, metaphysics, psychic and occult subjects generally.

Sun in good aspect: gives a very faithful or devotional and religious spirit.

Taken alone or afflicted: trouble in foreign lands; dangerous voyages (especially if in a Watery Sign); loss through legal affairs; troubles through relatives by marriage; self-deception, lack of comprehension of the profound or higher sciences or philosophies; likelihood of religious bigotness, and grave mental affliction.

Mars adverse: danger of serious mental derangements.

Uranus in Ninth House.

Troubles in foreign lands or through relatives by marriage; peculiar, unexpected or dangerous voyages; taste for philosophy, occult, metaphysical or unusual knowledge.

51

Original, inventive, peculiar, eccentric or reformative and progressive ideas. Desirous of traveling and investigating. Prophetic intuitive faculty and sometimes antiquarian or Uranian pursuits.

Neptune in Ninth House.

Clairvoyant or other psychic faculties; a highly inspirational nature; strange dreams, feelings and experiences.

Psychic studies or investigation of Spiritualism, phenomena and philosophy. Voyages if in a Movable or Watery Sign.

If afflicted: distressful dreams; ominous forebodings; troubles through travels; legal involvments; complicated affairs with wife's relatives. Adverse psychical experiences. Impressionable and simulative nature.

TENTH HOUSE.

Moon in Tenth House.

Inclines one to public life; changes in business, occupation and employment; instability of position and popularity; rise in life followed by reversal or downfall. Voyages if in a Watery or Cardinal Sign.

Women influence the position in some way, according to the aspects. If well aspected by Sun, Venus or Jupiter: favors success, popularity and prosperity. Carefulness in money matters and usually gain in property and possessions. Public business.

Mars adverse: public scandal or discredit; obstacles in business. Taken alone: it gives ability and tendencies to employment of a changing nature, shipping, voyaging, traveling, dealing in public commodities, novelties, etc., affairs connected with the common people and women generally, also with things ruled by the Sign occupied.

Mercury in Tenth House.

The honors, success in business or occupation depends upon the Sign and aspects, Mercury being neutral.

Good position for public service or those holding responsible positions under superiors.

publicity, in hospitals, institutions or in isolated positions, in remote, quiet, obscure places. Voyages. Mystery.

If the Moon is not in Scorpio or Capricorn and well aspected it shows development and progress, particularly through the occult.

Well aspected: success with large animals, ability for occult arts.

Afflicted: the subject lacks firmness and stability and is led into acts of indiscretion resulting in worry, trouble, secrets, and female enmities. Liability to restraint, enforced retirement or sickness in a hospital; fanciful fears.

Note: if the Moon is within 12 degrees above the ascending degree consider it as in the ascendant.

Mercury in Twelfth House.

Fondness for the investigation of occultism, chemistry, medicine, or secret arts and for risks and adventures of a secret or dangerous nature, for unusual lines of thought generally. Liking for mystery. Small worries and annoyances. Many small enmities, frequently caused by writing or scandalous reports. The subject possesses ability but lacks power or opportunities to manifest. Well aspected: tends to success ultimately. Note: if Mercury is within 12 degrees above the ascending degree consider it as in the ascendant.

Venus in Twelfth House.

Inclines to romance and adventure; a love for the mysterious in nature, for investigating the occult, secret arts, medicine, chemistry; pleasure and success with horses and other animals.

Gain by an obscure or plebeian occupation also benefit through charitable institutions. Peaceful or voluntary seclusion.

Secret love affairs, or intrigues leading to enmity of women; an early unoin (especially if Mars is in any aspect); affection for another after marriage, and, if Saturn afflicts, separation or divorce, and sorrow and disappointment through the opposite sex.

Scorpio, Capricorn or Cancer are the worst sign for Venus here, giving too great a love for physical and emotional pleasures, detrimental to the native because of excess.

61

Sun in Twelfth House.

Occult and psychic tendencies; uncommon tastes and inclinations. Seclusions, success over enemies, and success in medicine, chemistry, or occult affairs, also in some quiet, secret, obscure or unpopular occupation or in connection with hospitals; prisons or other institutions. Life in lands far from the place of birth. Help and charity received when needed.

If in a Watery Sign: strong mediumistic faculty.

Well aspected: the native is self-sacrificing and enduring and rises out of seclusion, obscurity or difficulties, by his own efforts, after the first third of life.

Afflicted: sorrow and misfortune through things indicated by the sign that the Sun is in.

Note: if within 12 degrees above the ascending degree consider it as in the ascendant.

Mars in Twelfth House.

Danger of injury, slander, scandal, loss of reputation or treachery from enemies or misplaced affection; grave trouble through impulse, lack of frankness or candor; liability to imprisonment.

Unfortunate adventures; secret enemies; danger of injury through large animals, and burglars. Death in seclusion or restraint. The partner is subject to feverish complaints.

If Mars is in Libra or Pisces it denotes poverty or limitations.

Saturn adverse: injuries or imprisonment.

Jupiter adverse: financial and social ruin.

Luminaries adverse: distressful circumstances.

The good aspects of Sun and Venus, or the Sign Capricorn here, improve this position of Mars.

Jupiter in Twelfth House.

Success in medicine, chemistry or occult studies; respect for ancient wisdom and teachings; success through asylums, hospitals or public institutions; through benevolence and philanthropy; in places remote from birth, in quiet places and with animals; charity given or received; the native readily helps others.

The subject prevails over enemies, they turn to friends and he eventually gains through them; reversals followed by success.

Peculiar experience in connection with the affections, which, however, results in benefit.

Aid from friends and others, quietly or secretly; success about the middle part of life.

Saturn in Twelfth House.

Well aspected: success in seclusion, or in quiet or laborious occupations.

Secret enemies who work for the native's downfall; losses and bruises through animals.

The nature is acquisitive, reserved, **and** inclined to quietness or solitude; desire to work secretly, unobserved, and to live peacefully or alone.

Secret sorrows, fears and disappointments; liability to false accusations and even imprisonment or confinement.

Uranus adverse: unexpected or strange enmities; disgrace, loss of credit and honor.

Mars adverse: danger of violence, robbers, or suicide.

Mercury adverse: liability to insanity, hallucinations.

Luminaries adverse: tendency to despondency; melancholia; sorrow through death of loved ones.

Uranus in Twelfth House.

Estrangement from one's native state or kindred; occult investigations; secret, romantic, mysterious affairs and attractions; difficulties with animals; psychic and magical experiences.

Afflicted: threatens disgrace; troubles through psychic and occult sources; eccentric, peculiar, violent tendencies; restraint in public institutions; mysterious and unexpected misfortunes; strange and unexpected enmities; eccentric people perplex and annoy by underhand actions.

Well aspected: success through occult affairs, institutions, etc.

Neptune in Twelfth House.

Well aspected: success in mediumship, psychical research and occult investigations; through secret, secluded and quiet methods, detective work, etc.

Afflicted: danger from psychic sources and through deception, schemes, fraud, secret enemies, scandal, disgrace and secret sorrows. Vague or weird apprehensions.

Astrology is the most useful science and the most necessary science known to humanity today. Astrology is the key to happiness in marriage. As Astrology becomes understood and used more and more, crime, warfare, failure, and poverty and sickness will disappear. It is the key to harmony. Because the horoscope of every individual is a guide and shows when he may use his senses, mind, strength and energy to avoid undesirable conditions and embrace those which are in keeping with progress and attainment.

"Once to every man and maiden
Comes the moment to decide,
Whether he shall rise and fluorish
Or in poverty abide.

"Once to every man and woman
Fate comes knocking at the door;
Once 'tis offered, once considered,
Once refused—it comes no more."

INFLUENCE OF ASCENDING SIGNS.

The following delineations of the effect of ascending signs are for the signs alone without any planet in the first house; if any planet be therein it will modify or accentuate these testimonies; if a fortunate planet, it will increase the good and diminish the adverse qualities, and vice versa if a malefic planet.

Whatever sign is on the first house of your Horoscope that is your Ascending sign.

ARIES ASCENDING—They admire scientific thought and are quite philosophical; do not become discouraged easily, and they possess a sharp, penetrating will power. They are at their best when they can guide, control and govern themselves or others, as they have the ability to plan and map out the future and lay out modes of action. They are lovers of independence, fond of their own way and happy only in activity and command. The desire is to be at the head of things and leaders in thought and action. They are enterprising and ambitious, quite versatile, and usually rather headstrong and impulsive; forceful and determined in effort and expressive in speech; intense when interested, vehement when excited. Somewhat inclined to be fiery or quick-tempered and ready to resent abuse or imposition and, while liable to go to extremes through indignation, they do not hold a grudge for any great length of time. They love justice and freedom; are enthusiastic admirers; have practical ideals, and possess an electric nature. The planetary significator is Mars.

TAURUS ASCENDING—Gives a self-reliant, persistent nature capable of working hard and long in order to accomplish their purposes. Gentle while unprovoked, but "mad as a bull" when really angered, and, when opposed are stubborn and unyielding; are usually quiet and dogmatic and somewhat secretive or reserved concerning their affairs. They have a great deal of endurance, latent power and energy; are practical and organizing and usually sincere, reliable and trustworthy. They are fond of pleasure and love beauty in nature, art, music and literature, and are moved a great deal by feeling and sympathy. Possessing a magnetic quality, they are able to benefit those who are deficient in vitality or those who are irritable or nervous. They are careful and steady and able to carry to completion the projects which they undertake. They have the ability to earn money for others and are good at all executive work, matters connected with the earth and its products succeed under their supervision. The planetary significator is Venus.

GEMINI ASCENDING—Makes one ambitious, aspiring, curious and given to inquiry, investigation and experimenting; they are also apt, dexterous and active and capable of engaging in two or more pursuits at the same time. The nature is sympathetic and sensitive; the mind is intuitional, perceptive and imaginative, also quite idealistic and fond of all mental recreation. There is a liking for pleasure and for adventure and for science and educational pursuits. At times they are restless, anxious, high-strung and diffusive; mentally timid, indecisive, irritable and excitable. They love change and diversity and must be constantly busy to be happy, because inactivity causes them impatience. They have the ability to become very clever, as they are progressive, inventive, mechanical and ingenious. They possess inherent conversational and literary ability. They do best in occupations where there is a variety of employment, where the mind and hands can be engaged in several different things. The literary and educational world is their best outlet. The planetary significator is Mercury.

CANCER ASCENDING—Gives a changeable, sensitive and retiring disposition with many changes and ups and downs of position and occupation. They have a fertile imagination, are somewhat sentimental, sympathetic and talkative. They are fond of home and family; are industrious, frugal, economical and anxious to acquire the goods of life. Fear of ridicule or criticism makes them discreet, diplomatic and conventional. They appreciate approbation and are easily encouraged by kindness. They have a tenacious memory, especially for family or historical events. The emotions are strong and they delight in beautiful scenery and in romantic or strange experiences or adventures. They have psychic and mediumistic faculty, are very conscientious, receptive to new ideas, and have the ability to adapt themselves to environments.

66

They are adapted to pursuits which embrace the catering for the masses and all matters of a fluctuating and public nature. The planetary significator is the Moon.

LEO ASCENDING—Gives a good-natured, philosophical, generous, kind-hearted, noble disposition. They are frank, free, outspoken, independent, impulsive, forceful and demonstrative in manner. Their nature is electric and inspiring. They have great hope, faith and fortitude, are energetic and lavish in the expenditure of energy and vitality when their sympathy or interest is aroused. In affection they are ardent, sincere and passionate. They are philanthropic, charitable, loyal, aspiring, conscientious, adaptable, inventive and intuitive; entertain high ideals; are imperious and fond of power and command; usually popular and leaders in their social sphere. They are generally good-tempered, though highstrung and quick to anger, yet are very forgiving and do not hold a grudge for long. They receive and grant favors readily and are usually fortunate in the long run. They succeed best where they have authority to hold some high or responsible position in managing or executive departments. The significator is the Sun.

VIRGO ASCENDING—This makes one modest, conservative, thoughtful, contemplative and industrious. They have a desire for wealth, but require extra effort to save money; are very active, not easily contented, and learn readily and quickly; have good endurance and do not show their age. Mentally, they are very perceptive and somewhat intuitive; are of a speculative turn and often give way to worry and over-anxiety; are sensitive to surroundings and to the conditions of others. They are quite discriminative and careful of details. Cautious regarding their own interests and will not neglect the interests of others, being diplomatic, tactful and shrewd. They are prudent, economical and practical and usually act with forethought. They should always avoid drugs and animal foods and should study hygiene with regard to diet to obtain best health. Commercial and business affairs and matters connected with the earth and its products succeed under their careful supervision. The planetary significator is Mercury.

LIBRA ASCENDING—Gives keen sense of perception with foresight and good comparison. They love justice, order, peace and harmony, and are usually very courteous, pleasant and agreeable persons, and although quick in decision and anger, are easily appeased. They are fond of beauty in all forms, in nature, art, music, literature, etc., and can enter with zest into refined and cultivated pleasures and amusements and greatly enjoy the company and society of brave, happy, sunny and mirthful people. They are affectionate, sympathetic, kind, generous and compassionate; also idealistic, artisitc, adaptable, constructive, intuitive, impressionable and inspirational. They admire modesty and refinement; are ambitious and dislike unclean work and all discord. The best outlet for their talents is in the professions, and they have ability for lines requiring good taste, neat touch or fine finish. The planetary significator is Venus.

SCORPIO ASCENDING—Makes one reserved, tenacious, determined and secretive, possessing a quick, keen, shrewd, critical and penetrating mentality. They are somewhat inclined to be suspicious or skeptical and stingingly sarcastic. They are quick-witted, quick in speech and action, and alert, forceful and positive. They are often blunt, brusque and seemingly fond of contest, but nevertheless they make strong and splendid friends. They possess grit and go-ahead-ativeness that will enable them to reach high attainments. They accomplish their purposes by subtlety, strength of will or by force if necessary. They have keen judgment and mechanical skill and much constructive or destructive ability. They enjoy travel, are fond of investigating mysteries and things occult; appreciating luxury, yet can be very frugal and economical. They are natural chemists, surgeons and contractors, and gifted in accomplishing things requiring muscular skill or aggressive enterprise. The planetary significator is Mars.

SAGITTARIUS ASCENDING—This gives a nature which is inclined to be jovial, bright, hopeful, generous and charitable. They love liberty and freedom, are very independent, dislike a master and will allow no one to order or drive them about, but are usually good-humored and honorable. In disposition they are frank, fearless, impulsive, demonstrative, outspoken, enterprising, nervously energetic, ambitious, sincere and quick to arrive at conclusions. They are sympathetic and loving, possess good calculation and fore-

He prefers strangers to relatives, is very generous as long as he can have his own way and cares much for pleasure. He is enterprising, makes large profits, and if careful will become very wealthy, and occupy high positions. He generally lives to a good old age, but has many enemies and few real friends. He is not easily excited, but very passionate when angry.

WOMAN—The woman born in this Sign is careful, studious, diligent and economical. She has many opportunities for marriage, but generally makes a mistake and is unhappy in domestic life. A lover, a divorce and a second marriage generally sets her right. She loves to give her friends good entertainments, but a stingy, miserly husband causes her many regrets. She is generous, freehearted, always ready to divide and always says just what she means regardless of consequences. When angered she smashes things in great shape. The favorite gems are the emerald and moss-agate.

Gemini People.

Born from May 20 to June 19, any year.

Gemini is a Variable, Hot, Moist, Masculine, Intellectual, Airy, Sanguine and Barren Sign. It rules the hands, arms and shoulders. Also rules friends and enemies.

MAN—The man born in this Sign will take many journeys through life and visit many places in search of fortune, yet he never becomes very rich nor able to obtain much credit. His many friends become enemies through jealousy. He is courageous and always ready for an emergency and generally squanders all he makes. He loves reading, is very fond of his opposite sex, fickle in his affections, but never loves more than one woman at a time. He is restless and uneasy, wanting to do something all the time and drifts through life following pleasure and fortune wherever it leads him.

WOMAN—The woman born in this Sign is generally very beautiful, good natured, easily influenced but honesty is one of her virtues. She has great wisdom, plenty of personal property and always takes things easy through life, although much given to worry. She is somewhat jealous but lives contented and comfortable. She does not believe everything she sees or hears, for if she did she would be very miserable. She is very seldom disappointed, as she has a powerful imagination and readily adapts herself to the various conditions and circumstances of life. The favorite gems are the amethyst and all high-colored stones.

79

Cancer People.

Born from June 20 to July 19, any year.

Cancer is a Watery, Cold, Moist, Phlegmatic, Feminine, Movable, Fruitful, Material Sign. It rules the chest and breast. Also rules health and life.

MAN—The man born in this Sign is inclined to be very vain, fond of dress and show and very fond of women. He is lively but worries a great deal at night and often falls into ill favor with his friends. He forgives but never forgets an injury. His early life is generally hard and wretched. He gets some property through marriage but never becomes very wealthy, although he never wants for anything. Death will seldom claim him before his sixtieth year.

WOMAN—The woman born in this Sign is quick to take offense, bound to have her own way but is easily discouraged if left alone. She is modest, will attend to her home, is economical and industrious, never minds inconveniences and generally marries more than once. She is destined to have many children and is very passionate and emotional. She always receives a large sum of money or property at some time during her life from some relative. She is very sensitive and kind hearted, has a good memory and is very conscientious in all positions of trust. The favorite gems are the onyx and emerald, which indicates success in love.

Leo People.

Born from July 20 to August 19, any year.

Leo is a Fiery, Fixed, Masculine, Barren and Material Sign. It rules the heart, blood and nerves. Also rules prosperity and losses.

MAN—The man born in this Sign is bold as a lion, a great talker, hasty; proud and sometimes very abusive. He is generally miserly towards his famliy, contrary and causes much trouble for those about him. He has many enemies and but few real friends yet he makes many acquaintances. He has good judgment, is a great borrower and inclined to be tricky and misses many good chances in life by not grasping his opportunities. He is generally long lived if not reckless and becomes more fortunate as he grows older.

WOMAN—The woman born in this Sign is generally very beautiful, courageous and virtuous. She is pleasing in manner and speech, but sometimes she will give her friends wrong impressions, thereby deceiving herself, not them. She is often loved and sought after but becomes irritable and indifferent and by this means her husband or lover becomes unfaithful to her. When aroused to

80

WOMAN—The woman born in this Sign is very fond of talking, is full of sympathy and compassion. She is good, honest and faithful in domestic life, refined and dislikes anything coarse, common or vulgar. She is destined to many children and a good old age. She is at times apparently stubborn, but easily coaxed, will worry without cause and does not show her affections as others often wish she would, as she is naturally timid and bashful. She generally marries more than once. The favorite gem is the amethyst, the symbol of temperance and chastity.

HEALTH

With the extremes in cold, dampness, heat, and wind, it would be advisable for every one to guard their health very carefully from now on, especially for the next three years. A noticeable increase in diseased conditions affecting the general health of people everywhere is indicated.

Patience needs to be cultivated, self control developed, bad habits eliminated, ways of living changed, and more thought given to service they can render to others, forgetting self, for we are on the border of a new and better era of existence.

Impatience, flying into ungovernable fits of rage, violent actions and intemperate ways of living, lay the foundations for diseased conditions to settle in our bodies and bring harmful results to the individuals who indulge in them. Intemperance in our habits, and mode of living, brings about an altered state of the blood, weakening the natural resistance of the body to disease. Hasty violent actions of any kind, particularly hasty speech, creates an inflammatory state in the blood, lowers its tone, resulting in attacks of an inflammatory, infectious and contagious nature. This should be remembered by every one.

CONTENTS

WS - #0056 - 301121 - C0 - 229/152/5 - PB - 9780282014742 - Gloss Lamination